WHAT MATTERS

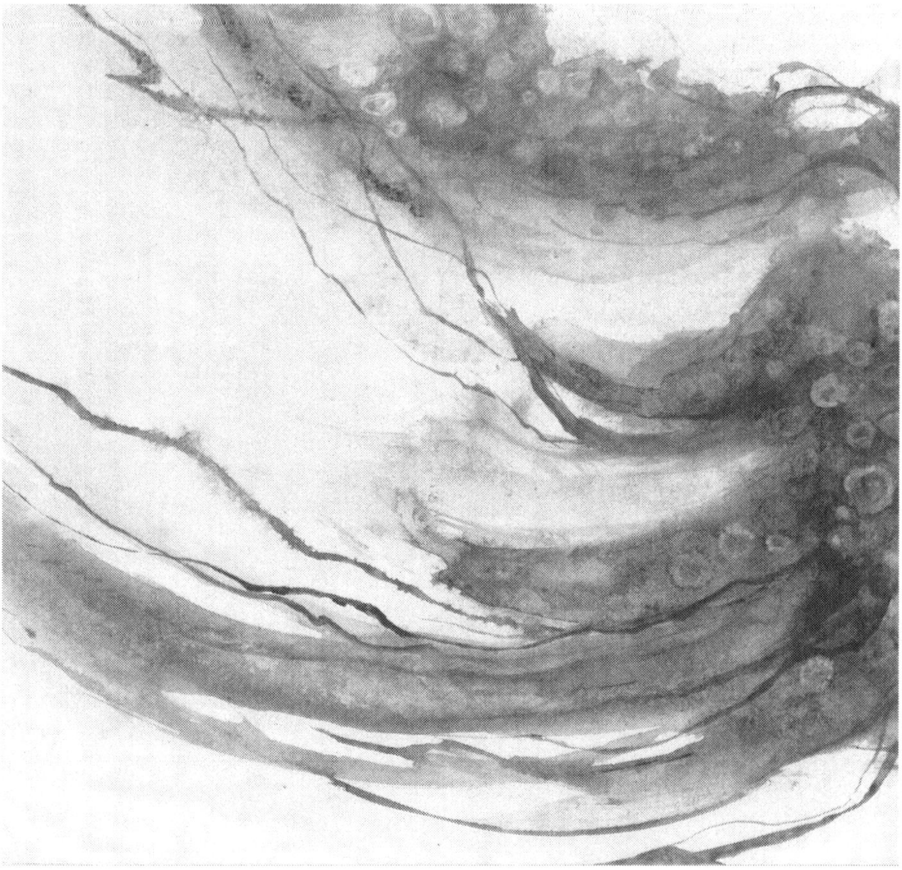

WHAT MATTERS

Reid Gilbert

Published in the United States of America by:

Imago Press
3710 East Edison
Tucson AZ 85716

Library of Congress Control Number: 2013945454

Book and Cover Design by Leila Joiner
Cover art © Wanda Hein

ISBN 978-1-935437-81-9
ISBN 1-935437-81-X

Printed in the United States of America on Acid-Free Paper

CONTENTS

This book is dedicated to the memory of my mother, Stella Mae Brinkley Gilbert, who introduced me to the joy of reading and writing poetry. Her favorite poet was John Greenleaf Whittier. Whenever my brother and I would bound out of the house…barefoot, of course…to explore the ridges and creeks and hollows, she invariably started quoting the first lines of Whittier's most beloved poem: "Blessings on thee, little man / Barefoot boy with cheeks of tan…" We would be too far away to hear how much more of the poem she might have remembered.

Her most quoted line of Whittier's was "For all sad words of tongue or pen, / The saddest are these: 'It might have been'."

MY RHYMES

2007

My rhymes at times are Hallmark cards,
But then like poems by Poe,
At times they're rippling mountain streams
And again are tales of woe.

Flitting like butterflies in a clear sky
Then heavy and down to earth
Some awash with tears in the eyes
And others with a touch of mirth.

TRAVEL MATTERS

ABOVE IT ALL

Election Day – November 4, 2008

Today, I'm above it all…
      literally…
      flying 37,000 feet
      above a nation of voters
selecting our leader
      for the next four years

a commander-in-chief, no matter which one,
      who will, no doubt,
change the course of history
      for us all
            as well as
      for all the rest
            of the world.

In what way he will change our fate,
      I wouldn't presume to know;
nor can anyone else
      despite the punditry of the commentators
            or even the promises of the contestants.

Are we all at the mercy of the economy
      with its infusion of bailout funds
            into the baggage of
                  personal and corporate and political greed?

Do we wait for the global temperature
      to warm our beds
            or scorch our souls
                with sunbeams
                    from heaven?

Will Grandpa's theological inevitability of destiny
        prevail
                despite our votes
                        and the best efforts
                                of the elected?

When I touch ground again
        for hope to remain alive
                it will be imperative
                        to hang onto
        the overhead straps
                for the wild ride through
                        the seasons and spaces
                                ahead.

LEAVING

Song for AT HOME script

No longer makin' a living
      In the hollows and the hills;
So leaving for the flatlands
      For work in the mills.
Weekends we'll be returnin'
      From wherever we may roam—
There's a strange strong yearnin'
      Toward the hills and for home.

Roads taken us from family
      Lead back home for sure
Even newer generations
      Knew where the real folks were.
Our neighborhoods and churches
      Or huntin' in the wood
Call like younger sweethearts
      To come back when we could.

The rivers and the branches
      Sing songs of quieter times
Of old folks still honored,
      Rememberin' deaths in the mines.
In new needs and good jobs
      We have mostly lost trust
Trusting now new promises
      Only when we must.

NEVER EVER

Santa Barbara, California, February 5, 2009

The impervious permanent rocky face of the of the mountain edge
      never exchanging its expression for years
            except when bathed with monsoon rains
                  or baking in summer's sunny days
                  or reflecting the beams of an All-Hallow's moon,
Looks down on the ever-traveling peripatetics
      uneasy in their restless rush
            forever without cease
                  streaming beneath on ribbons of concrete
                  or steaming away on the rim of the watery
                  horizon

Does he ever really regard us?
Do we ever really respect him?

Re-spect…again-to look.

How can we look *again,* if we haven't taken the first peek
      or regarded the visage looking
            down on us
                  from the rocky heights?

ARRIVAL BY AIR

air travel dis-encases my mind
soaring beyond the confines of the plane
past even the numinous sky
    deja vu
    images flying out of the ether
    while memories
    float through the clouds

why must I write in this metal cage

perhaps because I have chosen this route
and for the time being can be nowhere else
    isolated between
        there and here
        then and now

an unbodied voice announces
    our route has been modified
    our time of arrival has changed

it doesn't really matter does it—

    as long
    as I am
    in the air
        above and
        about everything

OUT THERE

At five in the morning
      on a cruise ship heading to India
         I look through the window
            for the mysterious horizon
Seeing neither ocean nor skyline.

Directed toward the black opaqueness
      my eyes focus only on the horizon
         of my own vaporous silhouette
Imaged on the surface of onyx glass.

Deeper in the mirrored window
      is a dimmed illumination
Providing light on figures behind me
      reminding me that
         I must wait for the rising sun
            to see
               what is
                  out there
                     before me.

AN EXCHANGE?

Traveling
        80 mph toward the east,
meeting other travelers
        80 mph toward the west.

They are going where
        and why
to do a job over there,
        or take something somewhere
        or meet perhaps a lady fair

Why don't I do your job
        and you could then do mine
I'll keep whatever I have
        which you could then decline
I'll visit your loved one,
        and you'll entertain mine

In that way when
        we share
no one will have to go
        anywhere.

BUT WHERE

Not there – but here
Not then – but now
Looking at the other elusive, clueless wanderers, as I ask,
      "Where are you going
            And from where are you coming?"

I open my ringing phone
      To retrieve a message for me.
         "Where are you going
            And from where are you coming?"

I teeter now
      I teeter at the edge
         Of a conspiring, deceiving unknown.
      I teeter on
         Antique, rubbery, unstable pins,
      But without
         A child's playful teeter-totter.

Now sitting at a green listless table
      On a teetering metal chair
         On a blocked-off triangle
            Of Times Square,
      And Broadway

Gawking at all the other teeterers
         Who come in all colors
         And sizes
         Donned in various masks.

CIRCLE OF LIFE

We circumnavigate the globe
        to return home to dig up the treasure,
buried there in the back yard.

It could not have been discovered
        without the circumventing trek.

Must I return physically to
        the place of my birth,
which, although still intact,
        has, itself, changed…
not the walls
nor the front steps
leading down to East 22nd street…
with ensuing years,
        encompassing other births
        as well as many deaths?

The soul has changed
        probably not for the better—
        hopefully not even for the worse.

Whether still standing
        in the same spot
        or sailing the seven seas,
the souls have continued to change
        some times to grow
        other times to atrophy.

But change they do;
        the starting point of place
        and the traveler of time,

still to remind
        that all circles have a center
                to rewind
and that the center requires
        strength with purpose
for the circumlocution
        and inclusive contents
to achieve the completion
        of winding up
                as well as
                        winding down.

LABYRINTH

Walking to the desert today,
I found there a stone-edged labyrinth.
I entered,
winding all the way to the center,
finding there a pedestalled ceramic bowl,
discovering then my only exit
was to reverse my course;
rediscovering at the entrance,
not a door,
but a doorway;
the way both in and out.

Psychologists put rats in a
maze, to
test their ability to emerge
then their ability to remember.

Did the Good Lord
put me here to
test my ability to emerge
then my ability to re-member…

    to member my present self
    to the identifying roots
    of my footprint
    in the mystery of the
    slough of my forebears?

EQUATOR HOMESICKNESS

Kerala, India
1966

white shirts
black umbrellas
white skirts
black feet
white sun
black train
white sky
black hills
all one today
all done today
black and white together
I'm going home today

PERU

a spiritual rush I'm still trying to decipher

spiritual hang-gliding in this ethereal air
is there danger of a crash
or a significant soft landing
        or no landing at all

the mural of the Christ in pastel draped robes
with an effeminate compassionate smile
is this the redeeming savior
or the sex symbol of all transgendered

to be alone in a swirling sea of unciphered language
is not for the lonely
but for the full of heart

when the speaker searches for the appropriate word
the terms he finds to use become more engaging
as the listener waits sympathetically and therefore
more attentive to every word and phrase

the surf lines its white head
against the sand edge of the beach
and clashes its symphony to the hills beyond

RIVERS

There are many rivers with which we must contend…
    fast moving rivers tumbling down from the hills…
    slow, sluggish rivers meandering through the plains.

Some are only riverbeds waiting to be filled…
    while others are rushing with dangerous falls.

Some with clear water, washing the rocks…
    some with debris from effluent lives.

Some we must ford, though it covers our boots…
    others carry ferries to hurry us along.

At times there are rivers flowing out of their assignments…
    flooding us with miseries of much too much,

Then there are rivers we sometimes must travel…
    floating along on the vagaries of the flow,

Or perhaps to swim against the power of the current…
    hoping to avoid the crushing cascades.

It seems that we never completely know the river…
    till we look back from the other side,

Or have traveled down the river to the very end…
    till we join the salt water of the ocean tide.

Why does it look so different when we stand here…
    than it did when we stood way over there?

A BLADE OF GRASS
Machu Picchu

To contemplate a blade of grass
      is to ignore its imposition in the ruins and rains
      between the monolithic sun and moon breasts of
      Machu-Picchu

Is to forget to ask it questions
      of why here and why now
      in this inconsequential place of nowhere
Or to allow it to ask its question
      of why it had to stay
      when the builders and worshipers left

It is to look beyond
      its slenderness
      its greenness
      its life-transporting veins,
          energizing its dance for the mountain gods
      its supple striations
      and even its song
          harmonizing in the symphony of the river
             cascading, crashing, clashing, clapping
             two thousand feet below.

If I can release the questions
      more especially the answers…

To contemplate *then* the blade of grass
      is to accept the gift
      of its dance
      its song
          in the universe
             of my own soul.

SHARED ROAD

There are times when words are never enough
    To chart the bends in the road up ahead,
And chatting can be just so much fluff
    To describe the steps already tread.

Whether roads converge in snow or not
    Or choice be made of a traveling mate,
One may confess with no sub-plot
    The meeting, itself, was a miracle of fate.

With no expectations, but hearts full of hope,
    We press forward with new interconnect;
Interstitial moments in their full scope
    Of lives now touched in mutual respect.

    Shall we travel merrily the road together,
    Despite clouds of inclement weather?

TRACY ARM GLACIER

the immensity of the particularities
      and the cohesiveness therein
comprise the vastness of the glacier
      the depth of the fjord
            and the profile of the granite

the raindrop doth not a torrent make
      and acting alone makes little impression
however when conjoined with similar chemical molecules
      reacting to forces of gravity
            they fill the crevices between the mountains

the single snowflake acting independently
      may inspire with its geometric lacework
but when clasping hands with sister snowflakes
      they amass the grinding glaciers who in their turn
            etch the features on the face of the boulder

the individual may impress with soaring accomplishment
      of earthly human achievement
but when cooperating with glacial forces of the universe
      we contribute to the preservation of natural inheritance
            and assist in the highest attainment of human potential

THE COWS

The cows stand
        huddled together
closer as
        the approaching storm
of snow with the wind
        plastering their tails.
No need to try grazing
        for green grass covered
with surfing ridges
        of drifting white
over the recent green
        hiding their trails.

Still cuddling their cud
        pressed quietly together
pleased because
        their bellies are full?
Satisfied
        because they're together still?
Contented
        despite inclemency of weather?

Or are they simply waiting
        for the evening feed
        when the warmth of the barn
        will meet their comforting need?

Do they ever wonder
        when they'll be part of the load
to way over yonder at
        their end of the road?

BETWIXT & BETWEEN

Foolishness and wisdom…
Wisdom is always a little foolish…
Only the wise can play the fool…
adequately.

On the Avocado Mountain
    we see the Atlantic and Pacific
        betwixt and between two powerful energies
          we're always betwixt and between
            there and here
            then and now
            them and us
            you and me

Costa Rica
    betwixt and between
        the old and the new.

Between the north bank and the south bank
        lie the crocodiles.

Between the action and the sedation
        lies the sensation.

Between the cacophonous human sounds on the bus
        and the mating cicada songs in the valley below our
        breakfast stop,
             I listen to the silence;
            with its own vibrations,
            which invite me in.

In the transitions of betweenesses
        we're never allowed to stop…completely;
        except for a few moments of
            Rest and Reflection.

Each moment must give way to the next transitioning moment,
        At 4:00 the beach moment is over

Between the bee and the flower is a harmony.

THESE ROADS AGAIN

To travel over these roads again
        is to revisit not only the road but the time.

And yet I see a farm that wasn't there twenty years ago…
        was it?

Of course it was;
        it's a hundred-year-old house.

Everything is so different and new
        and yet still the same.

The crops are still the same;
        the corn and soybeans.

And yet these are this year's crops,
        planted only two months ago.

The old crops have been taken in
        at the end of last year's summer.

Is life then only a new loop
        to be renewed with each new seeding season?

TIME MATTERS

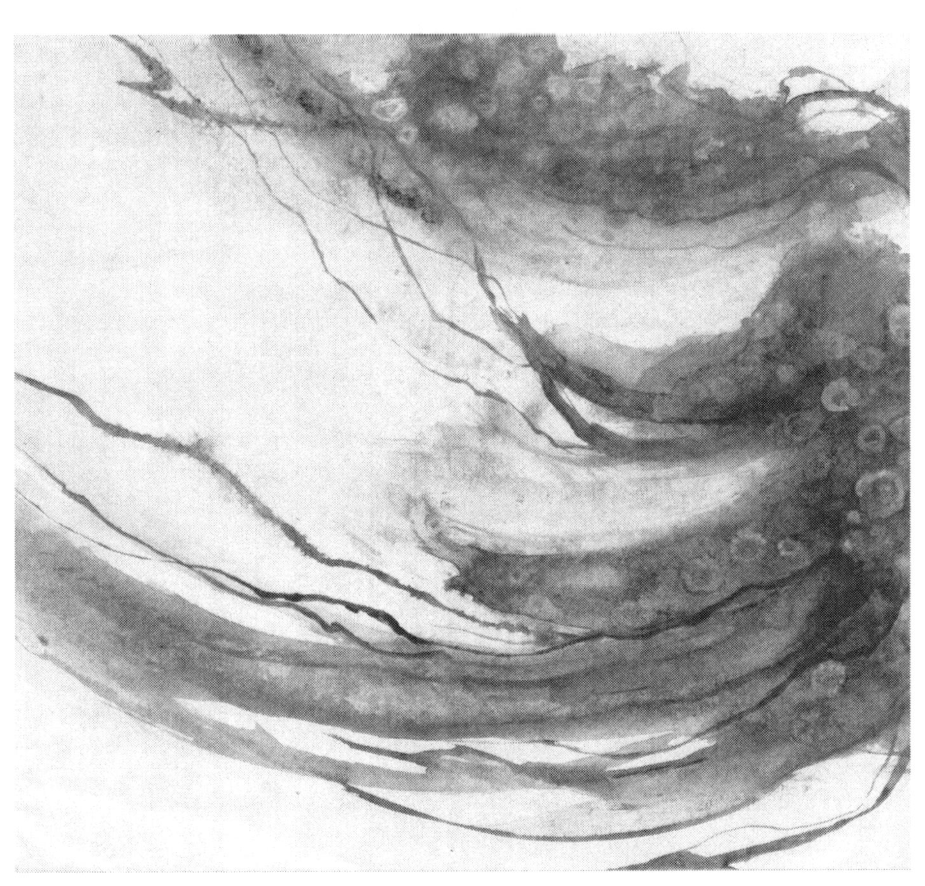

A MOMENT

I just need a moment
to catch my breath
and catch up with events of my life
which have brought
       NO
which have catapulted me
to this moment

the doctor's outer office
is soothing
with soft music pervading the air
pastel pictures enhancing the wall
of cactus flowers and new England hillsides
where everyone can feel at home back then

low whispers from other patients
being patient
while leafing through old
issues of newsweek
and time

now that I have rushed for the past half hour
as well as my past full years
I'll grab a moment
to doze
so drowsy
with nothing
disturbing
my empty
euphoria

that couple is leaving
after the wife enters the waiting room

from the medically-perfumed cocoon
of the doctor's inner sanctum
her lover helps her with her windbreaker
they push open the door
to re-enter their world

as they re-emerge in my mind
to see them as a
high school couple
with stars in their eyes
grit in their craws
but now they have digested enough of life
to revert to pabulum
and dessert munchies
a long way from their roots
but much like banyan trees
their extended limbs
have dropped new root branches
to new territory
enshrouding or perhaps
encapsulating new ground

my official name is called

Your Moment Is Up

COUNTING MOMENTS

We want each moment of our lives to count
     with purpose, significance and meaning,
     but while we worry and fret and pout
     the end must grow from the beginning.

The moments won't count,
     while we count them.
The moments will be purposeless
     when we pursue only that.
The moments are irretrievable
     as we try to retrieve them.
The moments remain insignificant,
     when we seek significance.
The moments retain little meaning,
     if we focus on mere meaning.

Each moment will count,
     when we stop counting.
Purpose will be there
     when we look elsewhere.
The moments are kept,
     if we let them go.
The significant moment
     looks beyond itself.
The meaning of the moment
     motions ahead.

Then when we shake off this "mortal coil"
and meet our maker face to face,
what will count without our counting
will be *how* we've run this *lively* race.

MY PAST PRESSES EVER

The past presses ever on the presence
of my present tense
diluting the intensification of my current life stream
while currently encapsulating any contemporary
happenstances it may now be confronting.

Thus my present mind deems this moment
increasingly sadly irrelevant
perhaps even enshrouded by any initiated
linear inner life invoked ere now.

The past seems to regard the present
whether dire or delightful
as even contemptuous
and certainly trivial
to my life of yore.

The question now intrudes upon
my conscious mind
asking what now impels my life force
into the future moment:
the renewed remembrance of past events
ever more real than the present
or the more recent experience
which one would think takes precedence?

Does the present transition into the new future
as everyone has readily assumed
or is the future simply informed by the ancient past
though we've been assured
it has already passed
into limbo
so long ago?

NOTHING NEW...

Santa Barbara, California
Feb. 3, 2009

The winged vulture riding silently on updrafts
      with outstretched wings
      embracing the warmth of the
      prevailing winds,
hoping to sense the sweet savor
      of the freshly dead,
has no more nor no less than
      the ancient bird of centuries ago—
          except for, perhaps, the gift of a recent roadkill.

The anonymous resident plutocrat inhabiting
      the obscenely expensive mansions above the valley
      yearning to experience the extensions
      of libidinous expectations
deriding the ghastly ghosts
      of the foreclosed weaklings,
has no more nor no less than
      the ancestors of prehistoric times—
          except for, maybe, the trappings of excessive externals.

THE SHED

2006

containing remnants of my life
useful and doubtful
mamma's old kitchen cabinet
minus the flour-bin sifter
with extended enameled counter
which I restored with paint
and a little extra work
on the drawer bottoms
but no one wanted/needed such
in the dispensing garage sale
also some extra-long natural-edge
walnut boards from the West Virginia farm
a few books rain-soaked
but which I attempted to save from
the thunderstorm during the sale
when I lost more than 500 other books
why had I saved the class list/grade book
from 45 years ago in India
great-grandma's oval framed picture
still there though concealed by wrappings
of impromptu cardboard
perhaps enough to keep her apparition
from spooking my daughters any more
other things like car wheels with tires
thrown in by someone else
an impressive rolltop desk which needs
to be put back together, but
as my daughter said, "That desk to me is dad"
though admittedly unassembled
the question remains how to dispense
with these trashy treasures
in a shed that belongs to someone else

TRANSITIONS

each moment transitions
        into a new moment,
but I am advised to grasp the moment
        carpe diem
whenever I make the great effort
        to "grasp the moment"
it escapes
        oozing out 'twixt my clinging fingers
        to transition to another moment

is my life a desperate attempt to
        carpe diem,
only to have it seep away into the
        next moment
which I grasp again
        to lose again
to be enticed once more
        to seek the stable moment

which itself melts
        beyond itself

without my volition
        or desire

VULNERABILITY

Does one dare expose
      one's vulnerability
when even trivia
      sifts the sands
when weekends extend
      into insomniac
and one's unsure
      what the message demands?

Does one attempt
      to retrieve one's pride
or can the old dog
      simply chalk it up
as his mixed signals are
      unfamiliar commands
when he's as shaky
      as a foundling pup,

When even questions
      go unanswered
except to be answered
      with newer questions,
and the words sought
      don't quite ring true
and go nowhere
      except as distractions.

One does wait for answers
      and attention
for important occasions
      like dentists and wars,
but may we also hope
      for pop-up toys
and springtime jonquils
      under midnight stars?

TO RETRIEVE A DREAM

To retrieve a dream
  don't clasp it too tightly
    but let it run gently
      through the hours of the night

To snatch a tip of the dream
  simply let it go
    like a mountain stream
      enjoy the music of the flow

The ripple of the moment
  has no chance to endure
    but ripples on
      to the watery overture.

CERTAINTIES

Certain certainties are certainly grave,
Presently presented in a presentational way.
Possibilities are possibly all that I have
With regretfully regrets of some previous day.

As I open the portals on all the tomorrows
What preparations do I prepare to prepare?
I must close the windows of old sorrows,
But what daring dares do I dare now to dare?

ONCE UPON A TIME

Staring at the blank pages of my mind
        while sitting at Machu Picchu
        where once the sun and moon worshipers sat

Once upon a time we, too, joined together
        in a community of God worshipers,
        then, for some reason, God disappeared.

Was He tired of us and left us alone,
        or did He weary and simply leave?

Or could we no longer justify or understand
        our indentured relationship status?

Now we feel desperate like Unitarians
        to find meaning to keep the congregation growing
        without the unifying force of a god.

If a god didn't exist, would we then have to invent one?

When I was seven I knew God existed
        because my teacher cared with a birthday cake.

When I was nine I knew God was…
        because of answered prayers.

I didn't need to analyze, question or quote;
        perceived by my childish eyes
        He accepted my childhood in its simplicity.

I write now to capture, trap, eternalize
        the internalized vision
        which so quickly fades.

LIFE HAPPENED

My life happened
      years ago

My life ended sometime
      tomorrow

In between dwelt angels and demons
      some of whom I trusted
Each however propelled me forward
      into new moments of breath

None answered my perplexity
      of the interstices of time and space
Or the bigger question
      of the infinitude of either

ALONG THE WAY

on the way out

Somehow already tripping out sans Leary or LSD
but exploring the quantum universe with Einstein
I've learned that I am that universe…
I am that history.
There is nowhere else but here
and every time is now.
So pay attention
and hold within…
thoughts which slip away as quickly
as they come to mind.

Everything now
along the way
is so familiar
—too familiar—
yet far from hand,
as I reach out and
touch every reality
as it backs away
from me.

This street is the one
I travel
often
these days
and yet the same dirt road
I trudged as a boy.

Well, tomorrow
will be a new day—
or
will it?

PHILOSOPHY MATTERS

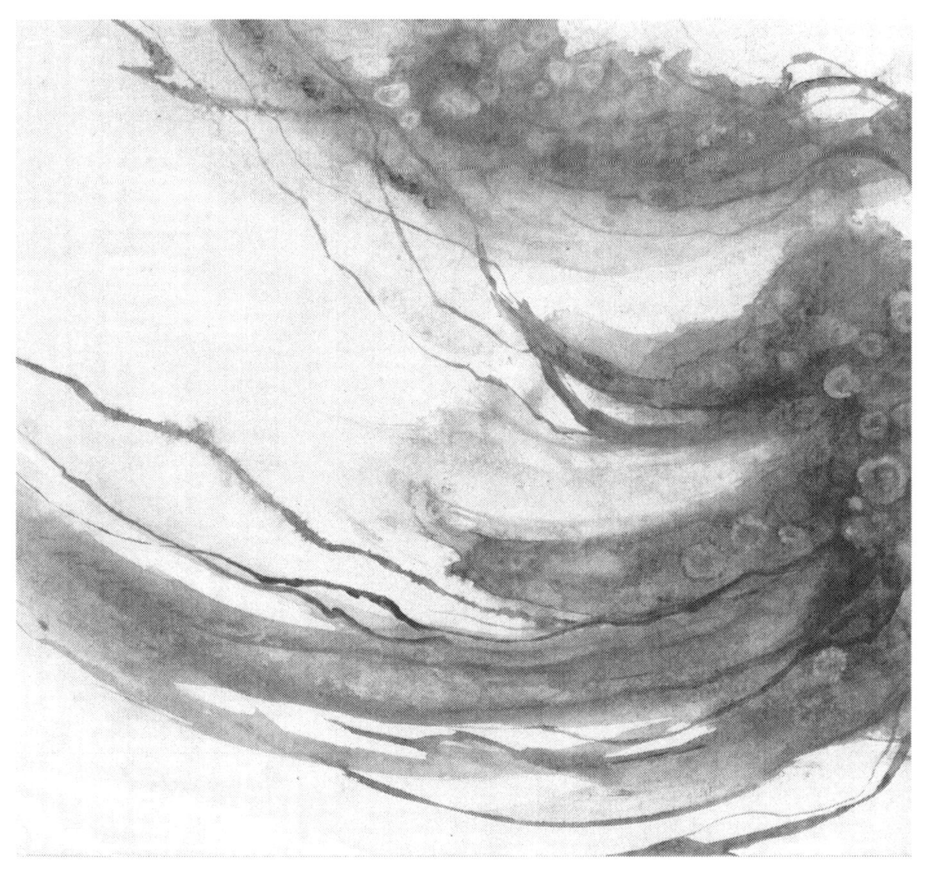

EMOTIONAL CLOUDS

Emotional clouds cover droughts with no rain.
And hover over my mind as dry as a bone.
But at four in the morning sleep muddles the brain
And ideas like swallows have frightfully flown.

Will they return to Capistrano by break of day
Or will they vacate for the entire season?
As I type down words with little to say,
I must've hit the erase button of reason.

SEDUCTIVE POETRY

2009

What do heartburns have to do with caring?
Perhaps to avoid sentiments too sweet.
Can't one just enjoy the time of sharing,
Even when life is not discreet?

Can one care too much and yet not enough
To make life-changing choices?
Does one have to deliberately snuff
Out of one's head all the inner voices?

Why is poetry seductive to write or read?
Perhaps in the attempt the heart must share,
As the poetic line unhusks the seed
One fears to expose to sun and air.

So I'll brace myself and try to be brave
And hope the words are not too grave.

HUMAN SEEDLINGS

The tree lifts its arms to receive the oxygen and sunlight
       from the universe
       as it sinks the rootlets of its feet into the earth
       for water, minerals and nutrients
              but this process is not an end in itself
              the tree exists in order
              to participate in and contribute to the universe.

Meditation is not a gift for me or for you
       it is an act of service for the sake of the universe.

Often losing our shared purpose
       we become so individualized that
       we suppose the universe is for us, individually, alone
              and we are dragged along by our self-centered senses.

Aristotle truncated the human focus when he made us aware
       that we were aware that we perceive that we perceive.

Descartes declared, "I think therefore I am."
       We capitalize I but not you or he or she or they or we.

These focuses of Aristotle and Descartes now cut us off from the
universe.
       Body parts don't exist for themselves alone
       but benefit and are benefited by the total body.
       Detached arms or hearts don't survive for long.

The raindrops and snowflakes of the Himalayas
       participate in the conglomerate to form the glacier which
       fills the crevices, etches the face of the rock and
       contributes to the initiation of life-giving rivers.

The individual acting alone is motivated too often by personal
fear and greed.

> Fear bombards from the outside and greed impels from an
> insecure center.

May the individual in concert move through knowledge to action

> participating in and contributing to the moving, living
> body of the universe.

I AM TIRED

I am tired
     of being blamed for your life-situation.

My birth as a white
     is not responsible for your blackness.
          I am tired of being blamed for being white.

My place of entering this life
     Is not responsible for your ethnicity.
          I am tired of being blamed for being an American.

My proclivity of sexuality
     Is not responsible for your sexual orientation.
          I am tired of being blamed for being heterosexual.

My endowment of genitalia
     Is not responsible for your sexual victimization.
          I am tired of being blamed for being male.

I am T I R E D

     Whenever you find me being unfair
          to your ethnicity
     Whenever you find me abusive
          to your gender
     Whenever you find me an obstacle
          to your sexual orientation:
               Chastise me
               Confront me
               Challenge me
                    But quit blaming me
                         For who you are.

I salute your ethnicity.
I commemorate your color.
I celebrate your feminism.
I respect your sexual orientation.

Please regard
My Weariness.

ON THE VERGE

We seem ever to be ever on the verge—
The interstitial merge between here and there
The never-never where between now and then
The Hamlet quandary when to be or whether

Although no longer in my teens
They seem ever to go wherever I go
And not quite now at death's open door
I feel the welcome of the grim reaper's breath

So ask me no questions of *ifs ands* or *buts*
The answers have been shut except at the curves
Where arrows point in several directions
And happenstances are forever endless

THE KEY

The key lies dormant as a door mat
under which it's sometimes secluded
until clasped by a human hand
with a specific task to be concluded.

To lock or unlatch the question may be asked
in dank dark or direct daylight;
so what is the project for this crucial object
to release or simply lock up tight?

Like a cloth to rub Aladdin's lamp
to give the gifts the genie chose
or to open the clasp on Pandora's box
unleashing numerous ponderous woes!

As the key locks up the vacated house
and locks out a love awash in tears
may it effectively unlock new affection
and gain strength through ensuing years.

Thus lives are opened or shuttered down
with some key wielded by a human hand,
but may the divine weld renewed lives
that transformed abilities may ever stand.

THE CANDLE WANES

Spitting

Sputtering

Spluttering

The candle

Drips and bows

Toward its holder

Who alas is its

Beholder

THE WAR

2006

The war growls and groans on
                    continuing to grow;
fertilized with further funds
renewed with broken bodies.

Filling the wards,
the haunted lives
                    as cannon fodder
                    from twisted lies.

Put on your mask, transforming you
as it transforms me;
                    but can it truly adequately
                    transform reality?

THERE IS MORE

There is *more* than this
but
you do not discover the *more*
by ignoring
or diminishing
or impugning
the *this* that is given

By honoring the *this*
the here
and now
one can find footholds
foundations
solidities on which
parapets & towers
can be erected
from which banners
may be flown

THEREFORE

And therefore this and that
       about what and whomever
is where and when
       one can know.

But to ascertain explicitly
       is to miss the point
of the event or the person who yearns
       so anxiously to be known.

Therefor there for the moment the known
       is as unknown as the unknown
while the unknown
       is as known as the known.

Thus to taint or taunt the tautological
       thereby twists the monkey's tail.

WE DON'T KNOW

To be perfectly honest,
we don't know
what we're talking about
but the point is
we have to
keep talking

So we keep listening
to the talking
wondering if the words
are mere prattle
or
words in search
of meaning

And who discerns the meaning
of
the voiced words—
the speaker
or
the listener

FOR THE REALTOR
2005

"Now straighten the stones
        in the paths
        and the walls.
Now replace the windows
        in the tower
        and the halls.
Now polish the floors
        in the foyer
        and the atrium.
Now pack up and pick up
        the bags
        in the kitchen.

"Prepare for the viewing,
        which will
        start soon,
As we schedule visitation
        tomorrow
        at noon."

I'm still a bit queasy
        in some self-denial.
Is it ever easy
        to embalm one's own child?

contemplating the vulnerable wren

plagiarism is to be avoided
to steal the words or the images of another is to attempt
to steal the other's self and thus lose one's own soul
however when reading
another's words one must delve deeply enough to
be writing the words with the writer
when observing another's painting
one must become the image in the painting
and guide the brush of the artist
when listening to the music of another
one must open not only the ears
but also the heart to dance the rhythm of the musician

to become so distracted as to become detached
or so immersed as though to invade
is to miss the point

my soul hopes to remain intent yet open enough
for the bird spirit to commune
as the bird flits onto the tree branch
the tree vibrates
to be touched is to vibrate
to claim credit is to discredit the event

time calls me back to watch the bird balance on the
grated fence
to balance he must fan his feathers
the tail feathers for staying
the wing feathers for leaving
thus we are in suspended animation
on the metal bar of reality

the wren usually the prey
is less frightened by my sentient presence
than the aggressive preying hawk
who keeps my inquisitive energy away from his comfort zone

I seek to appropriate the complementary rhythm of the birds
as the performer heeds the complementary rhythm of the
audience
or else we miss each other
in the dark

to make the invisible visible
is to let the wordless speak

COMFORT

When comfort extends itself into discomfort
where does one retreat for renewed comfort?
How can one become so comfortable
that it feels definitely *un*comfortable?
Is comfort merely a physical condition
or is it an acceptable frame of preconditions?

CERTAINTY

So little certainty
>   in the milieu of
>>   reality
>>>   so impure,

But one must act
>   as though
>>   certain things
>>>   are for sure.

This is true
>   of future reality
>>   we hope
>>>   will last.

May it not also
>   be true of
>>   aspects of
>>>   the past?

Was there any
>   certainty in
>>   yesterdays'
>>>   joys and sorrows,

And must today
>   always be
>>   the shorthand
>>>   of all the
>>>>   tomorrows?

CANDLE BOUQUET

The blue/yellow fire of the candle
ascends from the descending wick
arcing ever downward capped by a red glow
at the end of its slender black candlestick.

The flame reaches skyward
as it gestures to the side
opposite any passing object
which may cause a slight breeze.

Continuing its
praying gesture
the wick bends lower
with each consuming spark.

Set in the midst of a floral centerpiece
of multicolored cut flowers
looking very much alive
though their life lines now be numbered.

All this color of candle and flowers
with movement of flame and petal
mesmerizes one with the appearance
of the vitality of vibrant life.

Yet the sole part still alive is the flame
feeding on the shrinking tallow leaking
from the shriveling wick only to live
as long as wick and tallow give it life.

KING OF THE MOUNTAIN

King of the mountain could be played
on tops of haystacks or on beds
on rock piles or cords of wood
even up trees or mounds instead.

The kid on top could defend his position
with whatever weapon he might have found
and the attackers could all combine forces
in whichever way to bring the king down.

The U.S. has been king of the mountain
enjoying the prestige of the top
occupying it for a century and more
against an angry global backdrop.

Any kid knows when he descends
to strike preemptively those below
the top is undefended from other foes
and may even suffer a fatal blow.

I haven't forgotten my childish ways
and the thrill to bring the king flag down
but there may be new and different players
ready now to occupy that crown.

LIFE IS A REHEARSAL

Life is rehearsal for a dance
        that never happens?
        or happens only once?
        that happens often?

Surely life isn't a rehearsal
        for the life hereafter?
        the heavenly dance with harps?
        or the satanic dance with fire?

LIFE'S QUESTIONS

I ask the question,
>   but I don't find the answer,
probing into life's mysteries
>   to dredge 'neath the enigmas.

Must one then abandon
>   the search for meaning
as we attempt to focus
>   on one's ultimate purpose?

Is it necessary to
>   find all the answers
or is the question itself
>   sufficient to undergird our being?

The question will transport us
>   to the ultimate goal
even when we have no assurance
>   of where we are headed.

WELCOMED TO STONELEDGE

The neighbors were happy to see me
    the dogs were delighted
    when they recognized me
    after my extended absence of years
        Baby, the pup, had grown gray

The house was another matter
    with no welcome at all
    some windows were broken
    weeds approaching the porches
Two mighty hickorys had been chopped down
    their carcasses left to rot
    not even sawn up for useful lumber
    nor worked up for winter firewood

I suppose for safety of the house
    the trees were sacrificed
    standing so close
    in danger of falling on it in a storm.

But why would one feel the need
    to protect a house already dead
A house, like a large dead tree, may still stand
    though its heart has atrophied and
    stopped pumping life fluids to its parts
The lifeless roots may still clasp the rocks of *terra firma*,
    but their death-like grip can no longer
    suckle nutrients from mother earth's breast

Stoneledge may stand for a while like a deceased oak
    as a diseased testament to dreams and storms of the past

But with no collateral for vision of a future.

WEST VIRGINIA MOUNTAIN DREAMS

Song for AT HOME script

There are times in our lives
      When it mostly seems
That all we have left
      Are our hopes and our dreams.
They've taken our bodies
      To dig in the mines
With shovel and pickax
      Where the sun never shines.

They've taken our hands
      As well as our minds.
They've taken our lands
      Leaving little behind.
This is now not the life
      I thought that I chose
For my vision is gone
      As the day comes to a close.

The timber is gone now
      From the mountain ridgeline.
Even graveyards are covered
      With slag from the mines.
I'm afraid that they've darkened
      Our souls that were glad,
Even taken our dreams
      The last things that we had.

RISIBLE MATTERS

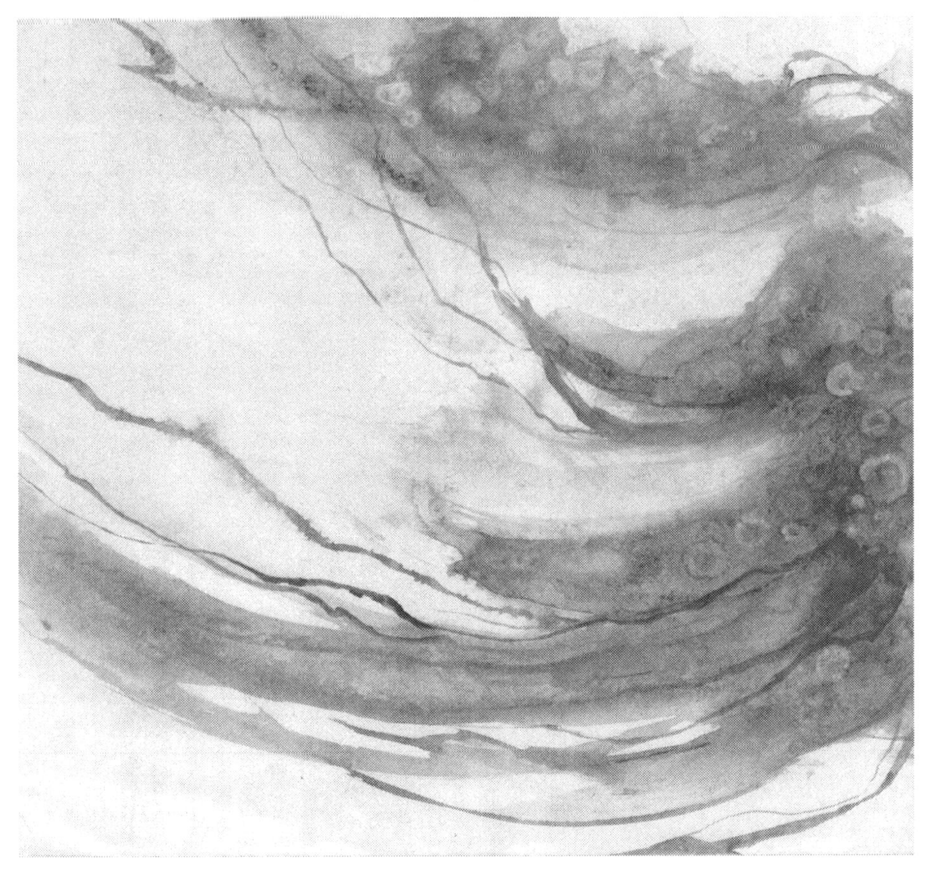

POOR SPELERS

A young lad wrote his lass a letter
Just to get to know her better.
      But alas the poor feller
      Was such a poor speller,
That he wrote he wanted to bed her.

The lass was miffed by the letter
But as a speller was no better.
      So then charming Freida
      Wanted him to be sweeter,
But wrote he should be into her sweater.

CEMENTIA

Words whiz through the maze of the mind of the clown
At times with a smile, but then a frown.
    It's the cementia
    Of dementia,
Which opens up when it closes down.

ODDITIES

The breeze that fans the new flame up
Is the same wind which blows it out.
The breath that cools the coffee cup
Warms the hands: there is no doubt.

HER PULCHRITUDE

May, 2008
(before Palin)

Her pulchritude

belies her attitude

of the certitude

of her rectitude

at the altitude

of her fortitude

in the solicitude

of her exactitude

ignoring the decrepitude

of her aptitude

but supplying multitudes

of pretty platitudes

not the beatitudes

of honored servitude.

AN EIGHTH GRADE DILEMMA

O please, Miss Jones don't call on me
       to trek up to the blackboard and conjugate
          the abstruse sentence chalked up there
          by you.

O, it's not that I can't conjugate and as you know
       how I always like to raise my hand to answer
          or go to the board to solve a problem
          or two.

It's just that today things are somehow different and
       much to my own utter surprise
New wonders have floated fancifully and even
       physically before my ravenous eyes.

Now I wouldn't want to show any embarrassing signs
       when currently in my juvenile distress
For Patsy Duncan just passed my desk
       and flipped at me the hem of her dress.

O what poor victim this mortal boy be
When angels arouse the blood in me.

DON'T TELL ME

Don't tell me I must no longer rhyme!
      Though a poet may still abbreviate
In this technological time
      it's frivolous to rhyme or alliterate?

Must I simply write a paragraph
      then break it up into
            little swatches
                  of phrases
                        and patches?

May I not use consonant plosives or sibilants
      with P's that ping
            and S's that hiss
                  or vowels that sing
                        like the breath of a kiss?

Oh, I understand that the old-fashioned rhyme
      is like gingerbread on a Victorian house,
So we'll leave the frills in this current time
      to the vagaries of a computer mouse.

CLICHES

Every word is a cliche
    If it has ever been used before,
But it will be known in no way
    If not used heretofore.

Thus the question arises (comes forth?)
    May leaves not be allowed to rustle
And won't there be a vacuous dearth
    When mouths can't gape and crowds shan't
bustle?

But we should leave well enough alone
    And wait to sing another day
Taking the literary path we've been shown
    To find another way to say.

AMEN

Eyes closed
Head tilted forward
Hands clasped in lap
Feet dangling off the floor
Rump squirming ever so slightly on the hard oak pew

Ears listening
Five-year old brain waiting
Waiting for the reverend voice to end
To end the prayer that called on the Dear Lord above
To forgive, to bless, to sanctify, to heal, to comfort the pew sitters

The end is always amen
But he hasn't amened his end
Others have amened again and again
Ol' man Styers yelled his amens over and over

Mamma taught that it was always rude
To ignore the feelings and suggestions of others
But the amens couldn't turn off the victrola
Of sing-songy long words directed heavenward
And the preacher of the morning didn't heed
The amen suggestions to end the longwinded prayer
Until a squeaky voice clamored a loud AMEN aloud

As silence hovered over the Sunday congregants

Closed eyes opened
Bowed heads turned toward me
I looked up
That cry for relief
Didn't come from me

Did it?

POET

To find oneself at the tip of time,
Standing there on the rim of rhyme,
Pushing words to fit a line,
Squeezing meaning to refine
A thought not fully there at the time.

Scratching now the scabs of the past,
Hoping new blood of old pains won't last,
Thus writing it down perhaps to show it;
That's when one would pose as poet?

TESTS

In this school of life
there will be many tests;
some at the blackboard
some at the desk.

One must measure the progress
to advance to the next level
with essays and multiple choice
pop quizzes and humiliating orals.

Then there are tests of true or false
with trick questions often thrown in
.

But why is it that each test given
always feels like the final exam?

AUTHENTICITY

What does physiognomy
Have to do with monogamy?
Need there be an apology
For basic biology?

And how is felicity
Affected by duplicity?
Is it the testimony
Of marital ceremony?

Where does parsimony
Fit in with matrimony?

It's just the simplicity
Of factual authenticity.

WHILE WE WAIT

What if the whys and whens and buts
Were bunched together in assigning blame;
Isn't there an onus to be put
On someone in this lifelong game?

I might as well claim my participation
And check all instruments for my GPS,
Then let my "well enough" alone
And forget the need to kneel and confess.

For who is monitoring my present condition
Mamma or Doctor or Guru or God?
While looking for someone, as I was told,
The absence now is extremely odd.

The person in charge here is Dr. Park
In whose waiting room I sit and wait.
I now assume my inherent right
To blame him for being an hour late.

ANOTHER WAY TO SAY

I've something to say
        or so I suppose,
but now how to express
        the something I chose

Perhaps in mime
        if silence were tolerable
or even in song
        if it were bearable

I could ensconce my something
        into a story of worth
with a final moral
        or a twist of mirth

Maybe a convoluted poem
        would suffice to impart
the something I need to say
        from deep in my heart

But I stand corrected
        of such a foolish notion
for poetry is too porous
        to share real emotion

Poems are meant
to string words together
or phrases with metaphors
as an abstruse tether.

And if you stumble
on words that rhyme

try children's books
when you write next time.

Ah foolish me I've forgotten
what I meant to say
probably just a frivolous
notion anyway.

OUT TO PASTURE

he's too old to pull a plow anymore
and that last colic spell
when he almost foundered
from his escapade in the green corn
nearly did him in

his mane is graying
and as he looks at you
with those rheumy eyes
one can only sympathize
and recall earlier stallion days

he was never a real racehorse
but he could run
and was never a Clydesdale
but could carry a load
and was always there when needed

so he's put out to pasture
we wouldn't think of
euthanasia
in deference for
his years of loyal service

BUT *I'M* NOT A HORSE

TO GO HOME

In college the accepted mantra was,

"You go home with him who brought you."

In congress the current mantra is,

"You go home with him who bought you."

I'M A MIME

Standing alone
Next to a grand piano
In the commodious ballroom
Rented tonight by the Fairfax Symphony

With cocktail in hand
Completely out of my element
Geographically, politically and socially

Another very special guest, unlike myself
A representative of the White House
Is also here
Surrounded by gaggles
Of grappling geese.

Knowing few people here
I am approached by the
Hostess of the evening
Whom I do know

"You must come meet people."

"Oh, I'm fine."

"But, you're standing here all alone."

"I'm a mime."

"What the hell does that mean?"

"I read body language, and I'm having a wonderful time."

She hastens to report her newest news
And blows my cover,

As they all turn their beaks
Surreptitiously to eye me
Out the corners of their
Lidless darkish eyes.

Then each begins a slow dance
Of adjusting longish necks
And repositioning webbed feet
While preening feathers
To assure themselves as well as
Any roguish strangers
That they are relaying the appropriate
Message they want
Or
Ought to be saying.

I read some fascinating
Defensives notes
And even some
Expressive epistles

Not from their original body language
Which I could hardly decipher
But their hurried, flurried protective
Memos tell me much
More than they would want
To broadcast
Or
Post on facebook.

Basically fearing
They are publically
Molting
Or their goose feathers
Are being plucked by an
Outlandish stranger.

PATRIOTISM?

Every morning in my schoolboy days
I pledged allegiance to the USA
Or to the flag for which it stands,
The proudest banner in the whole darn land.

Then a self-righteous reverend all pompous and proud
Wanted us to say "under God" right out loud.
We were already "under God" or Jehovah
Or Allah or Buddha or some divine ovah.

Why must we please a segment of the crowd
And wrap up in the flag as though in a shroud?
What happened to the phrase "We welcome to these shores"
People of all faiths, wealthy or poor?

Speaking of flags, I must confess
I waved the flag under no duress
Learned how in several triangles to fold it,
Also how to display and how to hold it.

Took it in from darkness or foul weather
We boys marched proudly with it together
Never would we dream ever to spurn it
But if it were dirty we must burn it.

The flag protocol has now made it right
For it to fly all day and all night.
All it needs now is an approved flag light.
Tattered flags on cars are a terrible sight.

Now tell me, dear patriots, if anyone can,
Does "under God" make me a better man?

And the lazy critter with an ever-burning light
Is he better than we who brought the flag in at night?

To respect means literally "to look again."
Thus my respect for the flag will ever remain,
But for us old codgers, don't set our heads spinning
With values we've held from the beginning.

RESPONSE TO

WISCONSIN UPRISING by John Nichols
2013

John I have finished your book
and in reading the last pages I read on p. 163
"…the failed fantasy that the United States could ever
be renewed by rapacious cannibalism."
Then putting on my specs I realized that I
had substituted cannibalism for capitalism.

Thinking further on the matter I realized
That my unbespectacled eye got it right.

My mind's eye traveled to my comic book earlier days
when I saw fat cannibals dancing around the fired pot
of missionaries being stewed for dinner.

My imaginative eye had no problem with reading
the names tattooed across the bulging bellies of
the capitalists…er…cannibals.
Koch…Trump…Limbaugh…Beck…Walker

As the whirling dervishes danced
the letters of the tattoos wiggled and squiggled
with the ever-expanding flesh of the midriff.

It was then I focused on earlier farm time memories
when the old cow or horse would get out of pasture
into the patch of field corn, in danger of foundering
themselves.

It would then be time to get out the Epsom Salt
to dose the farm beasts to prevent their bellies from
exploding.

Back to present day cogitating, I wonder
at what time the modern cannibals' pouches
will explode as they founder themselves
on all that green stuff.

Would a generous dose of
the Epsom Salt of Wisconsin Uprising
be able to stabilize the uncorralled beasts?

THE IMMINENCE OF THE IMMANENCE
OF DIVINE EMINENCE

November, 2008

Obama's political eminence is imminent,
But in some minds divine immanence
Hoping that the imminence of his political eminence
May facilitate the imminence of immanent eminence.

HUMANITY MATTERS

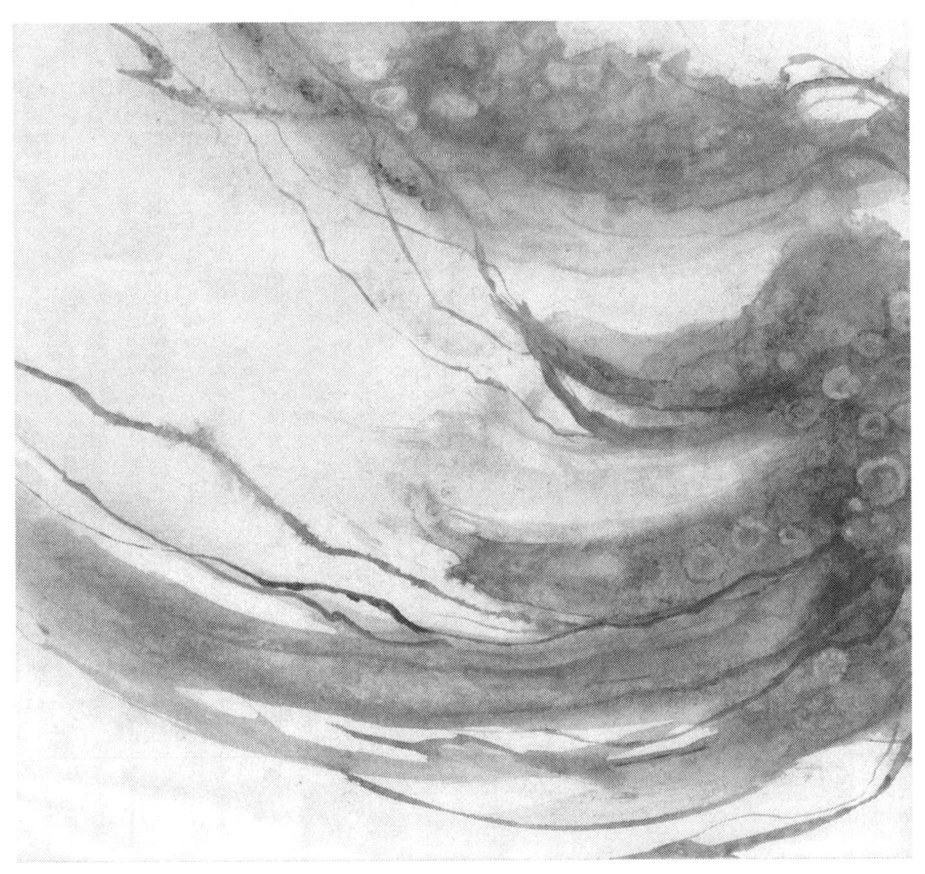

CHRISTINA TAYLOR-GREEN

(Born on 9/11/01, shot on 1/9/11 in Tucson, Arizona)

Dearest little star child

Whose bright personal light was bookended

By two national dark horrors of infamy,

Because you came we hope

Because of you we grieve.

We who never knew you in this lifetime

Miss you and your optimistic message

For an enthusiastic tomorrow.

CHILDREN OF INDIA

on a darkened street in
renewed New Delhi
a flute sang to me from atop a mound
of new construction dirt
voiced by a figure
I could barely see
a boy, perhaps six
who was unaware of me

in a crowded train station
in ancient Poona
with my compartment window
open to release the heat
I saw some children animatedly talking
when one came to me with sparkling eyes
to try out his English
one of his five languages

at a noisy village
South Indian rail depot
while starting my meal
of curried something or other
a small girl perhaps five saw my pale skin
and crossing several train tracks
lifted her begging bowl
for the opportunity for me to share

THE ARTIST

The artist can't really be depended on
        to fit into the establishment
        to color inside the lines
        to honor the norms of society
        to hold things in the accepted system
        to pay his debts
        at least on time

The artist can't be trusted because he
        enjoys himself
        doesn't hate his work
        asks too many questions
        avoids corporate creeds
        has little greed for financial reward
        even while expending great energy

He is a trickster who
        leads to an overhauling of our systems
        may even contribute to a diminution
        of the order of his art form
        is complicit with no compunction
        against the unnecessary
        leads us into roguery
        opens too many doors
        without closing any of them

He fancies himself in the realm of the divine
        without confessing
            or genuflecting
        outside the institution
            approaching Mount Olympus
                by simply involving himself
                    in a dance of creation

DAUGHTERS THREE

My daughters three.
Still listen for me?

Laughing at other men's tales
Sleeping to other men's songs,
Not always of my choosing
Whether right or wrong.

What happened to the all-wise
    Word filled questioning red-haired
    Petticoated frilly girl of my first fatherhood?

Where is now the sunshine reflecting
    Young one,
    Conspiring
    To invent a new Hindi-American language
    Known only
    To two three-year olds in the world?

And blue-belled blue-eyed dancing one,
    Butterfly still to tunes
        Tuned especially to you?

I now know the bedtime songs
    And chin-tucked sheets
        Were for old dad's assurance
            Of a safe night of dreams.

But still weep at the sad songs?
    Giggle at the funny talk?
        Cling at the fears of the dark?

FROM A SONLESS FATHER
1981

Fatherless sons
        To a sonless father
Sharing neither name
        Nor legal claim,

Fair-haired
Stair-stepped
Bi-cepped sons,

Intergalactic humanoids
Talon talented
Knuckleheaded

Sired before my entry
Birthed and loved by one
        Who once loved me,

Rocket into the
        Gaping maw of adulthood
                Looking neither back nor forth
        Nor out
        But in
                And therein fuels your strength.

Dear sons, never
        But, always mine,
Feather your engines
        For unfathering again.

THE WONDER
After the telephone call
6-15-69

The wonder
The wonder
Always the wonder
Of a flower
Of a heart

Grief
Rubs the soul raw
Then washes it clean

I picked two wildflowers
Today, Mamma, and tucked them in my overalls bib
For you
You would have planted them
And made them grow

You had a language I think
That we didn't know
And it coaxed
The bulbs to burst open
And reach to the sky
Where they unfolded
In a wonder
      of color
      of form
      of beauty

Today, Mamma
We seek that beauty
      your beauty
      in the world
      in the hearts

WHEN I ASK

When I ask kindergartners
>Who can sing?
>>All hands go up as humming begins.

When I ask kindergartners
>Who can dance?
>>All hands are raised as toes start wriggling.

When I ask kindergartners
>Who can paint
>>All hands wave as eyes begin to image.

Asking the same questions of the same children
>when they are high school seniors,
I encounter blank stares
>with a few timidly-raised fingers.

One may observe,
>"Something is terribly wrong with this picture!"

One may then ask,
>"What has happened in the educational process?"

I can tell what is wrong...

>The computer spellcheck has miscued...

>>It now spells

>>>CreatE

>>>>as

>>>CompetE

SHARECROPPER CHILDREN

Opal, the pretty one,
      swishing the tail end of her skirt
            at the city boys flashing by
      rumpled up in the rumble seat of their Model-A Ford

Beatrice, her older sister,
      already the unwed mother
            of a doddering woods colt
      the result probably of an incursion by their drunken daddy

Mabel, a younger sister,
      plain and bitter
            another school dropout
      wondering what she could do to get some longed-for
attention

Joe and Tom, two brothers,
      somewhere in the mix
            hadn't yet got their jollies off
      but knew how to climb walls and crawl into windows to
pilfer neighboring candy

Daisy, the youngest,
      had discovered
            the pure pleasure
      of finding little birds' nests and climbing up the tree to pull
off their little bobbling heads

Sharecropper children who shared few holy things
      but various dirt-farm pains

Why couldn't they begin
         or at least
              try
                  to stop
                        inflicting
                             further
                                  damage
                                       on
                                  themselves

Who will teach them

WHITE BOY WITH BLACK CORPSE

nearly sixteen that summer, I stood on the edge of a muddy pond
the swimming hole of the colored YMCA Camp Civitan
standing around with all the multicolored males in the area
waiting for the dam to be breached for the
water to empty into the creek for to
retrieve the corpses of two teenagers
who'd been frolicking with three others
in an unsteady boat, overturning while delivering
those two to their early watery graves

it would take hours for the emergency guys to arrive
and days for the pond to disgorge itself of its teatime
serous contents, both solid and otherwise

knowing that I knew how to swim and he didn't
my dad asked me if I thought I could go into the murky
water and retrieve at least one of the drowned boys
I said sure if there would be someone else to partner
in this humane gruesome task

the local white Pentecostal preacher claimed he could swim
but as he had a faulty heart valve and palpitations
he said he'd have to keep his head above water
but could hold the raft in place floating approximately
at the unmarked fluid spot where the mishap occurred

we stripped to our skivvies
surprising me that his checkered boxers
didn't have a picture of the suffering Jesus on the seat
I wondered why all the gawkers didn't also completely disrobe
then as we were all males we could see that with no clothes
we were all naked with similar equipment
just different colors and sizes

leaving the pastor clinging onto the raft
I descended into the unknown deeps of the opaque liquid
unable to see anything in the muddy depths
I brushed a corpse several times
before being able to grasp an arm
and surface with him to topside and the raft
where the disabled pious reverend waited

splashing our way to the welcoming shore
the raft, the preacher, the corpse and I
delivered the handsome black cadaver
to the outstretched hands of the unsegregated men
assisting us – white boy, black corpse and pious evangelist—
up the slimy red mud bank

that night – it was a Sunday – the reverend preached
loud and long about the unsaved teenage
boy whose knees quivered
— because he didn't know Jesus—
as he delivered the corpse of a black man
onto the shifting shores of a soulless, sin-filled sea

PANE OF GLASS

A pane of glass is just…
      well a pane of glass
it doesn't do anything…
      just stands there
caulked between four mitered
      ogee wooden moldings
transparently separating the inner world
      from the comings and goings of the outer.

For some it is more
      than a mere pane of glass
through inclement seasons of snow and sun
      separating the temperatures from in and out.

Elizabeth has looked through the pane of glass
      out over the little town of Belleville
but now when she looks
      she sees no one looking in.

Perhaps because her
      pane of glass on the second floor
is too high for anyone to
      peer inside.

No not stratospheric
      it's simply that at age ninety-six
         she is too old for anyone to care
            for anyone to care where she looks
      or for whom.

Eighty years ago she looked
      out the pane of glass

to see her beau
        walking up the path
                as he looked up at the pane of glass
                        to peer through it
for a special glimpse of her.

Seventy-six years ago
        she looked through
        the pane of glass
                to see the doctor
                        hurrying along
        to deliver her firstborn.

Sixty years ago she stood with lamp in hand
        looking through the pane of glass
                near curfew hour
        for the return of her young daughter
                who knew the way home because
                        of the light on the inner side of the pane.

Fifty years ago she looked through the pane of glass
        to see a son march off to glory
                and two years later
                        to see a soldier delivering news from the
                        war front.

Twenty years ago she saw the hearse
        arrive for the ride to the church
                her last trip with the
                        dearest on earth to her.

She now waits for the blessed angel
        who will escort her to the other side of the glass
                to be rejoined with those gone before

        to return to the womb of mother earth.

CATHARSIS IN TOBACCOLAND

1. The tobacco sharecroppers
    settled in again
    set up housekeeping
    burned off and cleared the newground
    broke land with the bull-tongue turning plow
    cleaned the plantbeds and sowed the seeds
    dropped the slips from the plantbed
    into the furrowed rows

2. hoed and weeded the crops
    gathered produce from the truck garden

3. cleaned the fruits and vegetables
    cooked the vittles

4. suckered and topped the tobacco plants
    pruned the orchard

5. poulticed weak backs and skinned knees
    alcoholed the chigger bites from berry picking

6. at night exchanged gossip and other word games
    even the meaning of scripture words

7. laid by (finished) the cultivated rows
    cradled and threshed the grain
    primed the "in order" leaves
    fired the hanging tobacco leaves
    in the tobacco barn
    tied up the tobacco leaves for market
    killed the hogs as cold weather came on
    gutted them for cleaning the chittlin's
    then firing up again for canning and salting away
    burned off the newground
    for the spring tobacco plantbed
    sat by the winter fire to clarify plans
    for next spring and moving on

The Greeks had a word, *catharsis;* presenting several images
    1. in one papyrus:"clearing" like twigs and stones
    2. in another papyrus:"winnowing" as in threshing of grain
    3. according to Diocles:"cleaning" of food before cooking
    4. Tehophrastus:"pruning" when cutting off extra growth
    5. Galen:"healing"
    6. Philodemus & Epicurus:"clarification," such as speech
    7. Chrysippus:"purifying" of the universe with fire

Do you mean to tell me that the sharecroppers were *cathartic*
all the while and didn't even know it?
    Were the Greeks also known as "po' white trash?"

GENERATIONAL DISARRAY

When this new generation somehow misses
      the earmarks appointed them for free.
I reflect on multifarious miscues
      an earlier generation provided for me.

When there were those greats and grands
      ahead of me many years before—
did they have any idea of what
      my world would have for me in store?

If only space and time would merge
      to listen to me for a while—
but I confess I failed to listen
      when I was yet still a child.

Perhaps generations could agree
      on a single respected dimension.
Might the quandary then be ended
      with no further apprehension?

ON THE SIDELINES

The mediocre man is always at his best.

Unwilling to risk failure or embarrassment
        we stand on the sidelines
        and hire dancers to dance for us
        and athletes to play for us.

Standing on the sidelines of history
        the white teenagers of Little Rock
        spat at and jeered the black kids
        walking stoically but determinedly
        into the future.

When the sputum of the mouths of the whites was
depleted
        their days ahead
        their future of influence and life
        had dried up
        leading them to blink unfathomly to ask,
        "What just happened?"

To watch the black football players of Ole Miss battle on
the gridiron
        against the black football players of Alabama U
        one may ask
        "Where are the protestors blocking James
Meredith?"
        "Does Bull Connors now roll over in his grave?"

The German Shepherd dogs of Selma were fortunate.
        They had no history and cared not for a future.
        Those dogs had their day
                and when night came
                the lights merely went out.

UNCLE ED

Uncle Ed Kaderly
not my uncle really, but hers,
was a successful Wisconsin farmer who drank too much
and swore as often as necessary.

For some reason the family: wife, sons, grandchildren, in-laws
were a little embarrassed by him,
though depending on him to maintain
their comfortable in-town lifestyles.

And I, a Methodist minister/teacher from the South,
who had married his sister-in-law's only daughter
was expected to shun him or upbraid him
or do end-runs around him at Thanksgiving dinners.

One summer I lost my pastoral appointment book
in the labyrinth of endless rows of tasseling corn,
where he and I looked for seemingly hours,
so that I would know where I should be when for the rest of
the year.

With no idea what such an appointment book may have meant,
he nevertheless understood the sense of loss of an important
appendage
having sacrificed two middle fingers of his right hand to a corn
shredder.

It was naturally expected when his family needed a clergyman
for his last rites
to request the professional services of a new in-law to "speak a
few words."

Having admired his cussedness and tenacious
determination,
I likened him to the strength and honesty of St. Peter.

When the "few words" were over, one of the sons
informed the undertaker,
"After that eulogy, I had to go up and peek in the casket
to see if that was really Pop in there."

THERE GO I

Donned in my recently acquired tropical attire of white *khadi*
I rode the enginely relic on an intricate pattern of lacework rails,
needling together various depots of the South Indian Peninsula.
I dared at the next watering hole to venture into local gustatory
    cuisine
despite warnings of dire consequences of ingesting anything
unpeeled or unboiled.

Scrunching to a screeching and clanging halt
the ancient locomotive screamed for its own liquid refreshment,
hissing steam, befogging all inhabitants on the station platform.
Station peons scurried from platform to compartments,
delivering meals to famished dusty and impatient travelers,
midst sloshing water from overhead reservoirs
as screaming little old men-like monkeys
outstretched demanding hands
through open train windows
for their own *baksheesh*.

Greeting my menu selection of rice and chicken *a la* something or
    other,
I encountered the eyes of a small girl approaching
from across several parallel tracks with her brass begging bowl,
which she lifted up through the window bars,
inviting me to share my sumptuous worldly feast.

Welcoming me into her malodorous world of human and spicey
    scents
and deafening sounds of train engine, monkey tribes and masses of
    people,
her silent eyes withered me small as her tiny hand repeatedly
slithered through the neck of her bowl and then to parched lips
delivering rare but welcome sustenance to an empty belly.

Still she stood there between the neighboring tracks,
continuing her shared meal of perhaps forbidden meat,
while watching this strange man from a foreign land,
as the train lurched me forward toward the next
destination.

With unblinking eyes
she moved her lips only to receive
the proffered nourishment.

I imagined an appropriate farewell
she might have offered:
There but for the grace of Vishnu go I.

HEART MATTERS

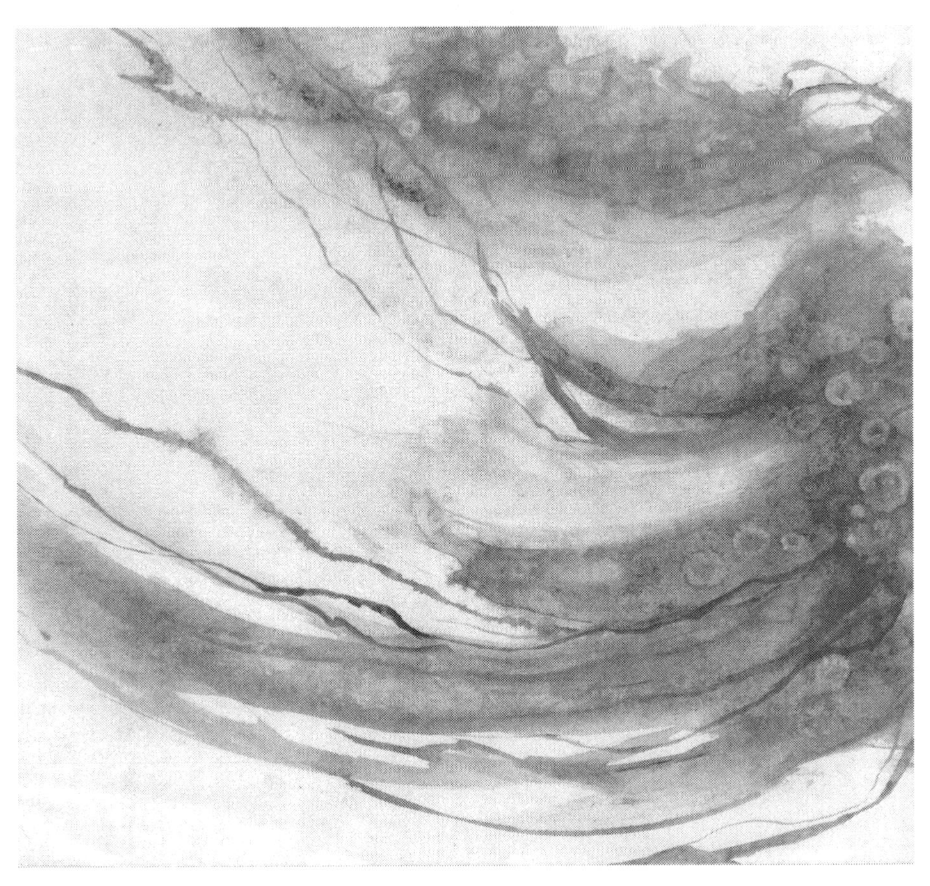

HOW DO I TELL HER

How do I tell her I love her?
      How do I tell her I care?
What are the words to measure my heart?
      What are the dreams that I dare?
Must our love now be only a mem'ry
      Will our dreams be pushed to the past?
Or can our old love now refreshen,
      And can our past dreams now still last?

Oh, I can now tell her I love her.
      I can now tell her I care.
These are the words that measure my heart;
      My old dreams I still dare.
Our love can be true and real now
      I hope I've found what to say
I ask her now to marry me
      That together we face a new day.

FOR EACH OTHER

It's when we start thinking for each other
       And correcting each others' facts,
I'll thank you not to bother,
       Struggling with my own syntax.

To beat up on myself is nothing rare,
       But I am not too deranged
To have someone else declare
       That I'm too stupid to know I'm strange.

As individual persons shall we take the chance
       To share life's joys as well as its trials
Or must we shuffle through a macabre dance
       To latch together the final miles?

Hand-in-hand would be a marvelous trip
       To trek through the bogs and hills,
But to be joined hip-to-hip
       Denies the discovery of the earlier thrill.

I STAND ASIDE

I reach my reach beyond my grasp;
           my grasp to feel your pain.
Your pain belongs to you alone;
           I cannot make it mine.

You own your pain I cannot reach
           ensconced in the self of your soul.
Yet your pain seeds a tree of infinite sorrow,
           whose shadow enshrouds my own self-
     spirit,
rototilling the roots of the Carcass Flower
           with its uncircumvented Priapus
           perfuming the canopy of the umbrellaed
     fog,
           bedding down
           in my Field of Poppies,
           memorializing long-forgotten detritus
                of lost hopes—
                dreams of something or other.

As you relive
           to relieve
           your hurt
on a trackless path
           which you now need follow,

I stand aside
     to sit alone
           on the edge of a ridge
                of hidden tears,

longingly looking
      across a sunless hollow
          to a love
              on the other side—
for you
      a bride now out of sight.

TOGETHER

We walked in the stillness
      of the silence of the night.
We talked of the silliness
      of the seriousness of life.

We sang in the meadows
      of hay, new-mown.
We danced on stone ledges
      of a dreamt-of home.

We bedded down in daisies
      in fields of youth.
We awakened on the crags
      of calcified truth.

CORNERS AND NICHES

There are corners and niches
Somewhere in one's heart
For old loves and losses
Though miles and years apart,

But there's always room aplenty
For new loves and new friends
As the heart never closes,
When it widens and expands.

A LOVE NOTE

I stepped to the door
And reached to knock.
It suddenly opened
And then I saw you.
We stood face to face
As though in shock
And at that moment
I was sure I knew.

It was then I knew
That I actually knew
Looking into
Your dancing eyes.
I knew 'cause you knew
That profound love
Is no longer
Just a sudden surprise.

THE DESERT

I came to the desert like a wounded dove
Much too tired to fly.
You welcomed me with wings of love
'Neath a canopy of big blue sky.

A rainbow is the logo of God's vow
Not to flood the earth again.
To fly we must open our wings and soar
Whether sunshine or in rain.

Should we fear next time the consuming fire
In the desert that has no green?
God will surely forget his dreadful ire,
When wings of love are seen.

the waves of emotional ecology

the radio waves of our being
  our beliefs sensations experiences emotions
    connect and are connected to those of all
  others
not merely to the individual *others*
  but to the mindset of our culture
  and the rest of the world
we understand that when one person
  punches another in the gut
    we grunt our own breath
      feeling the painful hurtful awful
  connect
but
  the greater connection is the
  psychic pain
    destructive
      even beyond
        this moment of
         time and
      specificity
the hateful word or thought becomes visceral
  to both giver
  and receiver

on the other hand
  a kind word
    warm smile
      caressing touch
  initiates
    a similar tide of
      ever-encircling
        concentric waves

to be shared
            narratively
                    intuitively
                            cosmically

these comprise the "emotional ecology"
        of our age

NEW LOVE FOR THE OLD

Your name pops up on the screen of my mind
At four in the morning, when I try desperately to sleep.
Can souls become lovers when the bodies haven't met
Commingling in the ether of cyberspace sheets?

When we share feelings and depths of thought
Of the experiences each has had in earlier years
What is love if not the gentle opening of hearts
With laughs and titters and not a few tears?

Leaving my earthly cot to commune with you
In words given to me from spirits above
We touch each other in realms of the soul
Resting in the assurance of reciprocal love.

Why have our paths crossed in electronic mode
When our younger lives had never met?
Are our eyes consigned never to meet
While in quantum space our journeys are set?

NOT THERE

We shared a moment
    You and I
With no words
    Nor even a sigh.

Words would have exposed
    The magic's charm
Or compromised the touch
    As to sound an alarm,

Of an implied promise
    Each of us had
Or exposed expectations
    Whether good or bad.

Only the sound of the music
    Of Beethoven…
        Or was it Acuff?

With crickets cricketing
    In the background…
        Or was it locusts?

With an occasional hoot
    Of a startled screech owl…
        Or was there no sound at all?

It was then I realized

    You weren't even there!

But then again

    Neither was I!

ST. ANTHONY

Can I retrieve things that I've lost,
If I ask St.Anthony for help;
All of the moments and all of the thoughts
That I've put away on a shelf?

What about the friends lost over the years;
Some whose names I no longer know,
And what of the innocence I thought I once had
Or the virginity lost a long time ago?

I know I've lost my heart to someone,
But I no longer want it back.
I think she's found it to keep it secure
In her own pretty haversack.

So I'll thank St.Anthony for the return of the keys
And other things of great cost,
But I'll thank him to keep his hands off
The heart that I gladly lost.

THE CHOOSER OR THE CHOICE
or
THE CHOICE OF THE CHOOSER

What choice can one make
      when one is chosen;
When at the door
      is the chooser's voice?
How can one choose
      not to choose,
When one seems
      to be the choice?

When the heart
      is open to a dance invitation,
Is it fair to one's heart
      whose gate opens wide,
To decline the dance
      sitting this one out
And close the windows,
      locking up the inside?

It's been a long time
      or so it seems
Since the last tango
      or an invite to the dance.
Does protocol matter
      when one finally chooses
To grab what could be
      a lost/last chance?

I now make the choice,
      though inopportune.

Yes, I'll heed the voice
      and dance the new tune.

WINTER-WITHERED ROSES

To: Whoever Stops

'Neath clouds, through trees, down hills, o'er ice-
encrusted earth
today I walked;
as instructed by poets, teachers, essayists and preachers,
as well as well-meaning friends,
I stopped to smell the winter-withered roses.

To: Whoever Listens

Looking 'round, I stooped down
reaching through thorny brambles
with glove-encased hands,
I touched ice-clad browned buds.
Pulling them to my nose,
I sniffed only frigid air.
Listening for songbirds,
I heard raucous caws.
Looking over the ridge,
I felt the stormy winds
with no voice from the rose.

To: Whoever Reaches

Tomorrow I'll walk again.
The ice will be melted.
The clouds will be gone.
The earth will be soft.
The winds will be calmed.
New buds will be opened,
     and then

I'll stoop again
to reach again
with bare hands
to touch again.

To: Whoever Hopes

Then I'll smell the roses
listening to the song.

SPIRIT MATTERS

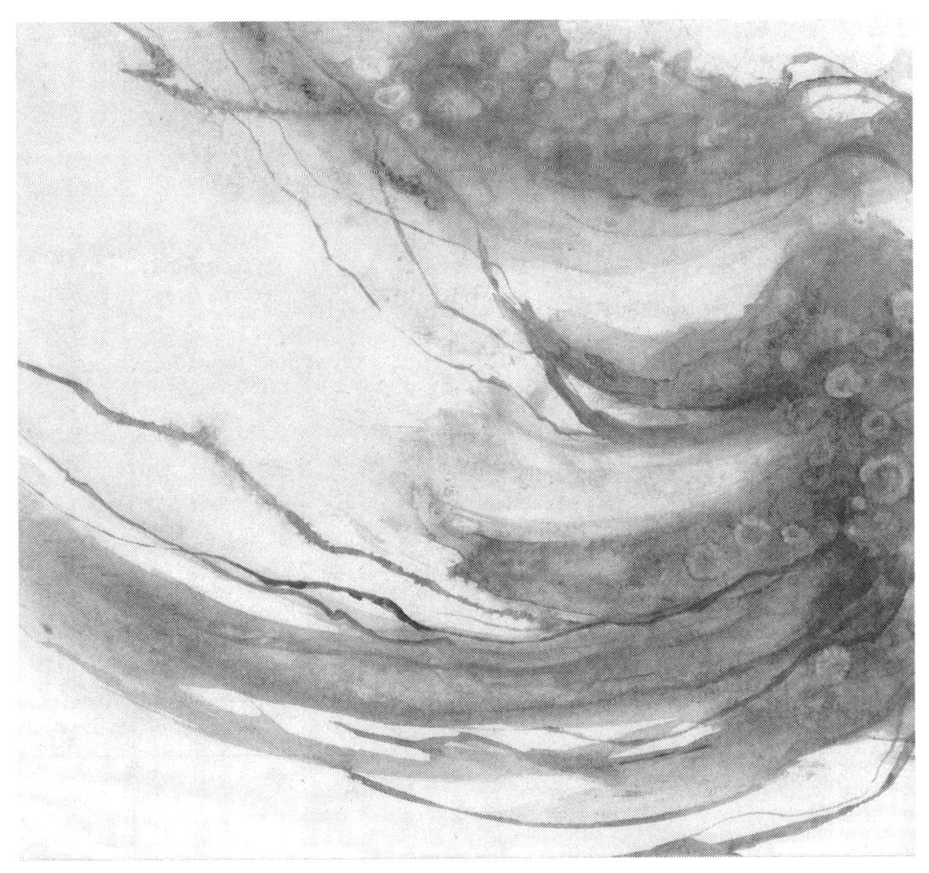

I DREAMT

I dreamt of playing Lear
      ranting and raving on the bleak hills of heath,
In regal robes all tattered with time
      with hoary hair blasting in bombast of wind,
Screaming against the elements
      and what gods there may be
With face besmeared and besotted
      by the tears of high heaven.

I awoke to reality
      of the part I'm to play;
The toothless, grinning
      smooth-pated Tuck;
A friar of benevolence
      in a tented nightgown,
Gathered at the waist
      with a clean, cotton cord;
Not the Lear rich colors
      nor a muddy soleless soul.

For I have received word,
      not direct, you know;
But via the circuits
      from the mucky-mucks

That I must cool it
And play my part
And agree to agree
With decisions up there.

For I must
      remember

Who I
         really am;
Not to pretend
         to grander parts.

In short,
         I must learn
To learn
         not to care.

THE CHAPEL AT DE GRAZIA

The De Grazia hand-built, hand-daubed, hand-painted chapel
        in honor of the Virgin of Guadalupe
Is always open
        with the front door standing ajar
And the aperture of the deliberate roof slit
        is ever receptive to sunshine, whenever the sun shines
                and to the rainfall whenever it rains.

Both sun and rain bathe and purify the sanctified floor
        of uncut stones from the desert.

As I sit on the rough-hewn
        last back log bench
My eye marches with the muralized devotees
        on the east wall
                carrying flowers and fern fronds
                        toward the angel harpist and cavorting
                angel band
Before turning the 90 degree corner
        toward the blessed holy virgin mother Mary
                enshrouded in plexiglass
                        protecting her from graffiti-artist vandals

As she looks down to accept
        and protect
                the devotional detritus of
                        photos, candles, beads, notes, figurines
        and for ever welcoming me
                whether on a regular basis
                        or after long absences.

She doesn't look in my direction
and doesn't need to.

There are few things which seem
to be everlasting
or eternal.

HANGING UP THERE

do you
      you hanging up there
            ever get embarrassed
with everyone ogling you
      you sometimes fastened on cross beams of rough lumber
            and then again on slats of gold
      but today floating off the lighted wall
            of the north end of a cathedral
                  embarrassed not really for your clothing
                        or lack thereof
            only a swatch of cloth
                covering your privates

why didn't they just disrobe you
      or why haven't you thrown it all off
            completely and shown the believers
                that you are *very man of very man*

you up there with no visible means of support
      not even a skyhook
            could now proclaim *very God of very God*
                hovering 'neath the heavenly canopy

no not embarrassed by any of that
      instead by having to tolerate
            those adulating minions
                genuflecting, bowing heads and
                    clasping together
                        their own hands

as they lift their eyes toward you
and through you to a father in absentia
and perhaps to the blood of a mother
never defiled by desire

what's the real difference between you the grim hanging man
and that round-faced fellow with a mischievous grin and
a tubby belly sitting cross-legged
on a cushion of stone

CONVERSION

Conversion claims a part of every conversation,
    For conversation doesn't truly happen
If some kind of conversion
    Doesn't take place,

Unless it is simply an exchange of words
    Or phrases from the top of one's head
Or from the jangling jaw
    Without impetus from the solar plexus.

But if it emanates from the heart
    Of both the speaker and the listener
From the giver and the receiver
    At least a minor conversion does occur,

Then the proffered spoken or written word
    Sits on the consciousness
If the gift of conversation
    Takes place at all.

The recipient of the word
    In the acceptance
Must deal with the utterance
    Be it harsh or kind or indifferent
Rehashing the word
    Reverberating its ramifications
Unable to erase it
    Completely from one's mind
Where it resides comfortably
    Or with a sense of unease.

GRAY GRANITE GRAVESTONE

Her gray granite gravestone stands seemingly alone
At the edge of the country church cemetery beside the deep woods
With the inscription, "Another flower in the garden of God"
But with no further indication of an anticipated spousal interment.

However, on her left, placed even before her arrival
Sits a small stone for an unexpected, premature first grandchild.
To her right is a ground-level marker for
The cremated ashes of her younger son
Having left this "veil of tears" with a little venomous assistance.

Between the granddaughter and the dark trees
Awaits a space anticipating the ashes of another son.
The two brothers of the same mother and father
As boys had rambled together the hills and crawdadded the creeks
Then traveled down different roads and across dissimilar waterways.

The younger son's stone proudly displays "PFC"
While the older son's stone will wear a "PhD".
Both brothers from the same hill farmstead
But each searching in his own way
For a world that made some sense.

DEATH IS MORE

Inspired by the life of Robert B. Graves
September 9, 2011

Death is more than passing over,
though it is that and yet much more.
It is a cessation of shared work and play
as we have enjoyed so oft before.

But there will be times in days ahead
when those of us left here behind
will remember past times of joy
vividly bringing those moments to mind

There will be occasions in the days ahead
when great wisdom will be received
by the ones on this side of the mysterious door,
as spoken to us like when he lived.

And as we lay to rest the mortal frame
may we be comforted by memories of his life
and now embracing each other in his name
be comforted in our present joy or strife.

GRIEF

       My!
How close to the shimmering surface
   grief lurks.

If only the waters were not so murky
   perhaps I would have seen
      and dealt with it
         peering up at me
            seeking my attention.

Would that the stream could simply
   wash down
      the lump of grief
         caught deep in my throat!

OM

to meditate
is an attempt to relate
the interior to the exterior

it is not to state
nor even to rate
which is inferior
and which superior

thus we substantiate
as we integrate
the disclosed whole
of the human soul

ON THE EDGE

The Great I Am
Comes to you
On the edge of asleep and awake.

Think without speaking
Speak without moving
Move without thinking

On the brink of breath and gasp
On the precipice of life and death

Twixt tears and laughter
Twixt heaven and hell

You

Will come

To you.

REFLECTION ON REPLACEMENTS

Transplants are replacements, are they not?
A transplanted tree replaces a tree,
Or does it simply fill an empty space
Where something used to be?
A diseased kidney or liver or heart
Needs a replacement, but whose will it be?
A prosthetic replaces, does it not,
A leg or arm with a new consignee?

But how does a person replace another
When the other's no longer there?
Is replacement even possible
Even when there's an empty chair?
Would one replace a worker newly fired
With another worker exactly the same,
Or perhaps a manufactured clone
Just identified with a different name?

As the British fired on the Gandhi followers,
And the first line of marchers fell,
When the next line stepped forward
To their own immediate hell
Were they simply replacements or new troops
Making their own personal choice,
Stepping ahead to face the guns,
Paying their dues of their own invoice.

Body parts may be transferred
And people may occupy a different space.
New recruits may resemble the old herd,
But the human soul can't be replaced.

WHAT OF IT?

What of
      the discarded chips from the sculptor's chisel
      the daubs of paint on the artist's easel

And what of
      the tales the teller left untold
      the words the poet failed to unfold

The marble of the Venus we continue to admire
But forgotten shards no longer inspire

What of us do they regard
What of us do they discard

What of them do we disdain
What of them do we retain

What of the poems woefully unneeded
What of the philosophies mostly unheeded

And what of God?

TO MEDITATE

to meditate
on one's fate
is to miss the now
and then somehow
get lost in the miasma
of conjectured obstacles
or oases not even on the hazy horizon
but on whirring wheels of fancy fantasies
and possibly even in the paranormal paranoia

to meditate
at this late date
of events left behind
as if now the need to remind
can somehow conveniently ameliorate
warped truculent images of polluted failure
or to languor in the hollow of a wrapped-up achievement
wefting even to wallow tenaciously in an unfulfilled
dream
never able to return or be transported to the
omnipresent moment

to meditate
while in this state
to focus on neither the
past achievement or failure
nor the future meditative fate
perhaps it's in the present moment
when the divine physician sutures both
the past and what lies ahead into the fullness
of mindfulness with the present attentiveness

METAPHOR

Metaphor is the mask of hidden meaning
        to understanding
                striking like a meteor to the heart of the matter
or rather perhaps a smokescreened
        dysfunction
                diverting to a meaningless pool of backwater
                irrelevance.

Masks reveal the true character
        or deliberately divert the focus.
Pantalone wears the mask of Pantalone
        not that of Arlechino.
Arlechino doesn't wear the mask of Brighella,
        unless he does so as a trick.

Anything can serve as metaphor
        to mask or unmask
something else—
        elucidating, exploring, examining
                or perhaps
        encrusting, eluding, evading.

Fences may be metaphors for limits or boundaries
        for hostile
        or protective
                purposes.

When I call a spade a *spade*
        does that metaphor
                reveal
                    or
                conceal?

O LOVELY WORLD

Schubert, "O Lovely World, Where Art Thou?"

"O lovely world, where art thou?"
> A question with haunting potential
>> A riddle with no answer
>>> And yet cosmic implication.

The riddle encased in still another riddle or two.
> The *kundalini shakti*
>> The power of consciousness
>>> A coiled snake with heads at each
> end.

Why ask the question if we know the lovely world exists
> By having seen it in spatial dimensions
>> Or sensed it in momentary awarenesses?

How can we ask the question if we haven't seen it
> At least obliquely
>> Or perhaps dimly?

Is that lovely world an external phenomenon
> To be photographed
>> In a moment of time
>>> Never to be repeated?

Or does the loveliness exist internally
> Without quantifiable properties
>> But with depth of understanding
>>> Uninhibited by vagaries of time?

The question continues to haunt
> Because I know the lovely world is there
>> As it seduces
>>> Any creative efforts.

It continues to taunt
>Because I know my attempts to experience it
>Will never be adequate
>To capture it.

It is inspirational indeed
>To know the lovely world exists
>Even as we acknowledge
>Its effusive elusiveness!

SO CLOSE

June 29, 2011

Standing at the stove
     while death is so close
Preparing my food
     despite the end of a life
But sustenance must
     continue to be addressed
Even when nearby death
     feels ever so small
While I ask myself
     is death ever far away
And food now is
     somehow rather tasteless
Perhaps because
     eternity lies so close by
But I keep telling myself
     it's such a little death
However for the mouse
     in the sprung trap
Its cataclysmic ending.
     is such a big thing.

THE KILLING

Song for AT HOME script

Old Othello wondered aloud
       What to do with his wife.
"How many ways shall I kill her," he said,
       "To end this damnable strife?"

So the desperate man asks the same,
       To end a turmoiled life;
"How many ways shall I kill myself,
       With poison, rope or a knife?

"The world will neither heed nor care
       The choices that I have,
But what will my children wonder about
       The griefs I take to my grave?

"While I'm released from the trials of life
       And escape at the end of a rope,
I'm afraid I'll bind them for generations to come
       And poison their own personal hopes.

"I'll simply do whatever I must
       With the life given to me.
Then I'll take that life any way that I can
       And trust to eternity.

"What they'll do with the lives they have
       They'll also do what they must.
I pray that the memory I leave to them
       Will not be a burden, I trust."

PITY ME NOT

Pity me not,
      Be not so unkind.

Note not
      My incapacities of
           Physical functions

Nor excuse
      My excessiveness of
           Eccentricities.

Life has now become
      A new reality
           Seemingly unrelated
              To past
              Or future.

Rather both
      Of which
           Enfold into
              While hovering over
                  And undergirding
                  My

                      NOW
              When everything matters
                As life thrusts itself
                Into my
                  BEING.

DOESN'T MATTER

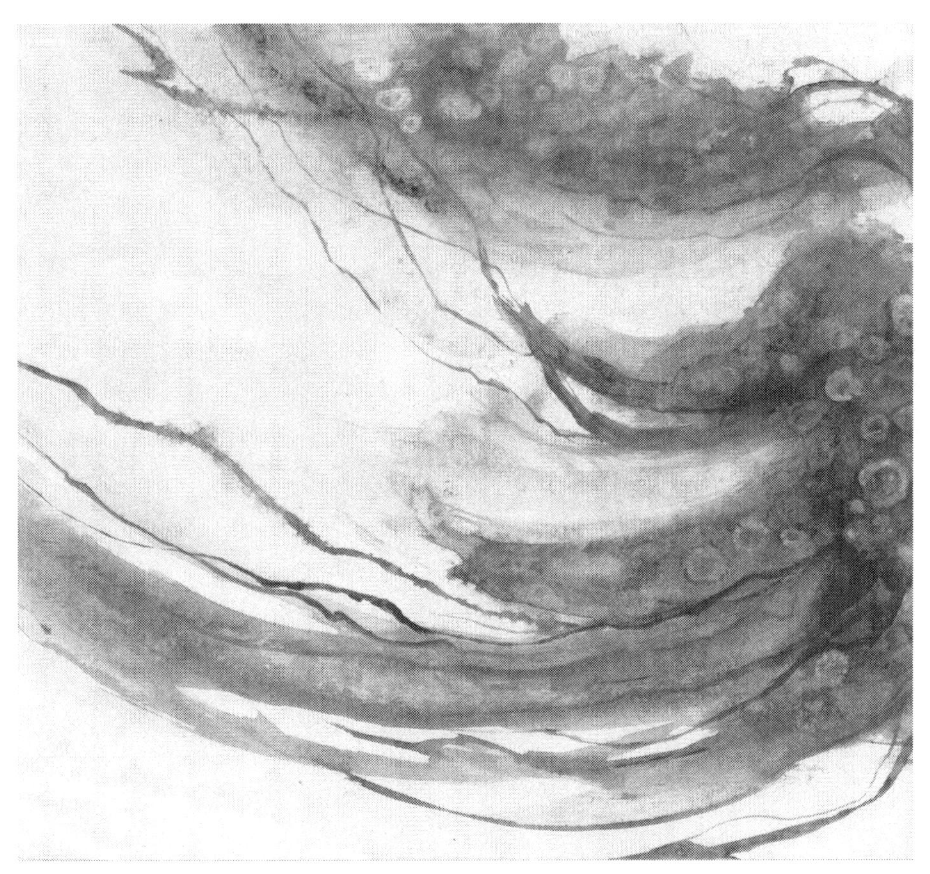

TILL IT DOESN'T MATTER ANYMORE

I'll keep on going
>Till it doesn't matter anymore.
And doing and making
>Till it doesn't matter anymore.
I'll sing and dance and breathe
>Till it doesn't matter anymore.
To walk and run if necessary
>Till it doesn't matter anymore.

Somehow now it doesn't hurt so much
>*As it doesn't matter anymore.*

COVER GRAPHICS

Wanda Hein has exhibited her paintings (water color, oil and acrylic) in juried galleries throughout California and Arizona for more than seventy years, achieving many awards and honors.

ABOUT THE AUTHOR

E. Reid Gilbert grew up in the Appalachian foothills of North Carolina, which have served as the roots of all his writing, not only in these poems, but also in his previous books, Trickster Jack and Shall We Gather at the River. After finishing high school, he received academic degrees from Brevard College, Duke University, Southern Methodist University, Union Theological Seminary (NYC), culminating in a PhD in Asian Theatre at the University of Wisconsin. He served churches in New Jersey, Indiana, and Wisconsin. His teaching careers included Union College, Lambuth College, and Ohio State University. As Founder and Director of the Wisconsin Theatre and School, he also served five years as Administrator of the International Mimes and Pantomimists. He was the recipient of two Fulbright Awards to India and Thailand.

CPSIA information can be obtained at www.ICGtesting.com
Printed in the USA
LVOW13s1918060913

351160LV00002B/8/P